Season of the

Sorceress

Poetry and Prose

Praise for Season of the Sorceress

I had the honor of pre-reading this glorious collection of poetry from a powerhouse poet of fierce truth. Highly recommended for your first 2019 poetry purchase of the year.

- Candice Louisa Daquin, Pinch the Lock

Reading *Season of the Sorceress* brought me heart-deep into the kind of poetry and prose that wakes us up and creates space within the soul. Melody's work reveals the beauty of words in a deep, earthy way. My witch's heart was captured without apology. Each story, each poem took me further into mystical imagination. There is integrity and passion on each page, but more than that, there is raw freedom of expression, which makes for a truly memorable book. If words are magic, then Melody knows how to cast a spell. The rhythm of the seasons, the mystery of the elements, the truth of vulnerability, and the strength of memories collide between the pages. *Season of the Sorceress* inspired me and left me thinking of possibility; and that is what great art is all about. Wildly recommended.

- Monika Carless, *The Dark Pool Trilogy*

Each section of this beautiful compilation is stunning in its own right, each encouraging me to dig deeper into my own being, to rummage around in her words and my heart and draw every beautiful strand of my essence to the surface.

Melody talks to the woman in me, the spirit in me, the fire in me and not only touches my soul, but all the streams leading to it. She has an innate ability to remind me of my strength, the beauty in developing it and the artistry in building it into my life.

I walk away after reading her work, always, with a deeper understanding of everything sacred both within me and within the natural world that surrounds me, and reading her work is nothing short of magic, when she leaves me feeling as if I have spoken to the stars themselves.

- Rachel Finch, *A Sparrow Stirs its Wings*

Other Books by Melody Lee

Moon Gypsy, A Collection of Poetry and Prose
Vine: Book of Poetry

Season of the Sorceress

Poetry and Prose

Melody Lee

INDIE BLU(E)
PUBLISHING

ISBN 978-1-7328000-3-8
Library of Congress Control Number: 2019935123

Editor: Christine E. Ray
Cover Design: Mitch Green

Dedication

This book is dedicated to my mom and dad.

Katie Maye,
I think many
of the poems in
here will help in
your healing. We
are all stronger
than we realize
and trials — even
heartbreak — make
us even stronger "Woman,"
Read "Broken hearted Woman,"
Page 33. In Section 4,
"Butterfly and
Growing Pains."

Much love,
Melody
4/1/19

Foreword

If you are an avid poetry lover, you have purchased this book with the intention of embarking on a spiritual journey. A few hours of self-care delivered the *only way you know how.* And if you're already a fan of Melody's talent, then you're settled in, licking your lips as you begin to turn the pages. Primed and ready, you know this author speaks your language. But if this is your first offering, be prepared to have your heart and soul lifted and transported by way of lyrical bites of poetic thoughts and powerful flowing prose. Melody has crafted something quite levitating with this third book of poetry *Season of the Sorceress.*

Melody has the ability to create imagery that uplifts and cajoles her readers into believing we are capable of anything, regardless of our personal circumstances. Empowering, her rhythm and beat will reach the places within you that have slumbered undisturbed because they were never inspired to throw back the covers with inner strength and say, "I can."

With lines like: *We were letters lost in translation / read under sheets with shaky hands / and trembling tongues,* you know the poem **Letters** will unearth the romantic in you but turn the page and you will find edginess and bohemian spunk. We get to see the core of Melody's craft and the marrow in her bones within her poem ***Roots***.

I come from the makers...those known to spark controversy. You know the ones, those edgy bohemians...the artists, painters, writers...dreamers...gypsies...misfits...rebels...the libertines. The creative ones labeled trouble makers. The thinkers and the doers. The outspoken. All in my blood.

Many of her poems are filled with cathartic twists and magical wisdom and are told in such a way that you feel like you're sitting down with a bestie eating confetti birthday cake and sipping white wine. She pulls you in and presses you to the curve of her neck and you hear her whisper: *"Me too."* That is a talent that every writer hopes to portray, and Melody executes it flawlessly.

There are thousands of writers that we have the privilege of reading on social media today, but I can say with absolute conviction that few have acquired the skill that Melody conveys in being able to tell a story with such depth, within the condensed form of poetry. Her brazen pen paints brushstrokes, making you feel a lifetime within a few carefully created lines.

This book is a mesmerizing feast for the rumbling that echoes from the poetic soul and there is little doubt that *Season of the Sorceress* will sate your hunger. It is a must for your poetic library.

Alfa, Bestselling Author of *Abandoned Breaths* and *I Find You in the Darkness*

Table of Contents

Section I

Fireflies

And Then It Hit Me

The house I grew up in was burned down to the ground by its new owners. The neighbors presumed arson due to the *gorgeous* new home that was quickly rebuilt, but lack of evidence kept the new residents free from conviction.

Even though I no longer lived there or even visited my hometown, learning of the fire greatly saddened me. I left my home town years prior to this incident, and when my parents and brother eventually left also, I never went back; never had a reason. My personal philosophy has always been, the past is the past, over, gone, why revisit it. Any therapist would likely tell me, you revisit the past to heal, and Melody, you will never heal if you don't go back. But besides the occasional family reunion, which is not even in my home town, I don't go there, physically or mentally, and not too often the latter. I left the past alone in an attempt to make a better life for myself and my children. So far, a success, I don't care what any professional says.

And then it hit me, the symbolism of the burning…and rebuilding.

3

Growing Up

They played inside with dollhouses
and toy kitchens.
I played outside, in the woods,
climbing trees, building forts.
They liked Barbie dolls. I did, too,
but I especially loved my Darth Vader doll.
They laughed at me; Darth was for boys,
the troubled ones, the kind of boys I gravitated
toward in life. The kind I would eventually
fall in love with.

They watched sitcoms. I read books.
They doodled. I painted.
They kept their dainty hands and fingers clean.
I got paint stuck in my hair and clay embedded
under my nails.
They got prim, tidy and pretty.
I got muddy, dirty and beautiful.
They learned to hide their flaws.
I learned to be proud of mine.

Musings

I read something written by a 19, maybe 20-year old. I was in awe of her young wisdom, her insight, her honesty. Her words resonated, profoundly touching a part of me I had not visited for quite some time, a place deep inside, an emptiness I thought I had filled. This young woman, whom I don't even know, except through her writing, reminded me of an old soul living in a young shell. I think back to when I was her age, 18, 17, 15. It is difficult. I don't know that girl anymore, that part of me that once existed. She is not me. Long gone.

I have come a long way since the decades between then and now, since those foolish teenage girl years. I can barely remember her and I don't want to try. I don't relate to her, we have nothing in common. Nothing! Save our blood. I suppose if I had kept diaries back then, like I keep journals now, I would have oceans of stories and poems, because at 18 I *was* that old soul living in a young shell, but my mind and body were young, reckless, naïve. I was living on my own at 18, thinking I was badass. And I behaved in that idiotic 18-year old way. I don't like 18. I could not do it again, would refuse to return…Oh god, the anguish of that year. Thank the lord that is way in the past and I never have to go there again.

But then I had a dream, a vivid dream—I was 15 years old sitting on the slide at Carpenter's Park kissing the first boy I ever loved. And he turns into another boy I loved. I am 14, downstairs at my house (the one that burned to the ground)

5

kissing another boy I crushed on, until he decided we were both too young to be hung up on each other and he went to his next teenage conquest. Then, I am 18 again, living with a boy I naively thought would be the answer to my pitiful 18-year old problems. And we loved and we fought and we loved and we split.

I have lived a full life. I have loved and loved. I have scorched for love. I have felt the pain of love and the joy of love. I have done stupid things for love. I have loved to the point of madness! And this other person I used to be but to whom I no longer relate, *does* have stories to tell. Maybe I did keep diaries all those years ago, maybe I burned them, too.

Beautiful Messy Love

Real love is always a bit disheveled
and if people tell you it's not,
that it's peaches and sunshine,
roses without thorns, they are lying.
Either due to ignorance or they have never loved.
I may not know much, but I know a thing
or two about real love and I promise you,
the best ones are full of messy imperfections.

Melody Lee

Go Deeper

Don't simply gaze at my cover.
Lick your fingers,
peel back the pages,
read the love between the lines
and the soul inside the words.
Keep reading until you feel my spine.
Allow my entire essence to coil
around your mind.

Nocturnal

I fall in love so easily
with rhythms of the night
moonflowers
wolves
vampires
things that hunt
things that bite.
I fall in love with scars—
their intricacies
stories of survival,
of courage and strength—
the way some fall in love
with hearts,
for I *feel* beauty
where others merely see marks.

Melody Lee

Quintessence

Souls don't know age,
race or color.
Souls only know
feelings, connections, love.

Reaching

My soul found you in the dark last night,
found you in my dreams.
I was reaching for you,
giving you my all, my body, every crevice
of my heart.
You did not understand,
so, I firmly, yet tenderly, cupped your face
in my hands, piercing your eyes with mine,
enunciating every word dripping off my tongue,
pleading for you to comprehend,
but sometimes in dreams, as in life,
all the explaining in the world
won't reach the other, if the heart is not receptive.

Melody Lee

Letters

We were letters lost in translation
read under sheets with shaky hands
and trembling tongues.

Crimson tears soaked our pillows
as burnt, rusty leaves
swayed in the deep heat of summer.

Even the softest breeze
was never meant to remain
on any branch
or under a single tree.
Wild things eventually leave;
they scurry, scamper…
They fly.

Words become fabrications, seductive lies.
Dishonesty crumbles,
deteriorating into nothingness,
because it was never real to begin with.
July, August.

Summer turned to autumn
and we both scampered away,
disappearing into the horizon.
You and I, we could never quite reach
our utopian castle, high in the sky.

Finding Myself

Getting lost in someone else, tending to their needs,
neglecting your own, you can only do that for so long
before you begin to lose yourself. Self-care is critical
in order to care for others and send light to the world.
Finding yourself in someone is different than
getting lost in someone for too long.

I left you, so I could find me.

Melody Lee

Wall

Every time you shut her out
she loved you a little less
and pulled back a little more.
Don't put this all on her, you
taught her how to build a wall
around her heart. You showed
her how to use her wings
to fly away…from you.

My Greatest Fall

You were winter,
I was spring.
You gave me cold days,
I gave you warm nights.
For a while our contradictions worked,
eventually, though, we became disharmony,
it took a toll on my heart,
so I moved on to summer,
letting you become my greatest fall.

Melody Lee

Autumn

Autumn
time like resurrection
where old things pass away
reborn in new light,
like Lazarus
where life falls to death
rising again in brand new skin.

Season of the Sorceress

The season of death and decay,
October, November,
some say dark and morbid,
yet I am rejuvenated, energetic.
For me, autumn is about vitality,
leaves waltzing in the wind,
vibrant fall colors everywhere. Life! A celebration—
bountiful harvests of pumpkins, apples, squash;
violet skies; cooler days and fresh, clean air.

Everything seems electric in the season
of the sorceress.
Longer walks; less sweaty, less fatigue.
Ravens watch over me, while I play
in orange and yellow leaves, hug dancing trees
and drink from the witch's fountain.

I am more alive in autumn than
in the heat and humidity
of summer, the frigid winter,
or the resurrection of spring.

Gossamer Wings

Raven butterfly
gossamer wings
ethereal
delicate dancer
pirouetting
in celestial dark
tiny bird
vivacious
fierce
fluttering about
rebellious
unbound
free…

Omnipotent

Darkness cannot consume those filled with meadows of flames, galaxies of stars; it can never touch fire, it can only be swallowed in it. Darkness is fearful and weak, filled with illusions and deceptions. Light is omniscient, omnipotent. Light is power, energy, strength, truth. You are the sun, constellations burning fiercely. Be so dazzling in your raw authenticity that hearts cannot help but stare and darkness cannot help but flee.

Melody Lee

Crystalline

She had the kind of heart
that made you feel safe.
The kind that's impossible
to forget. Big and pure
and beautiful.

My mom.

Roots

I come from the makers…those known to spark controversy.
You know the ones, those edgy bohemians…the artists,
painters, writers…dreamers…gypsies…misfits…rebels…the
libertines. The creative ones labeled trouble makers. The
thinkers and the doers. The outspoken.
All in my blood.

I Am but a Branch

I have an ancestor who was accused of witchcraft in the 1692-93 Salem witch trials for being true to her heart and speaking out against such nonsense, instead of sitting back passively while others hung for crimes they did not commit. In those days, women did not dare deviate from their expected paths and roles, lest they be an outcast, labeled "witches," sent to trial, condemned to jail, some even ultimately hung (men as well, for that matter). My roots go deep; they are sprouting from the earth, pulsing with life, a force from a different realm, flowing like lava in my blood. On my left, spirits guide; they even have names, my beautiful secrets. On my right, archangels protect. I am but a branch on the artists' tree still growing, hot liquid flowing through my veins.

Inheritance

Ancient wisdom flickers
behind sharp eyes,
these untamable torches.
My bones
deposits of inherited bravery.
I am a proud descendent of strong,
courageous women who went to the stake
fighting for their truths.

Melody Lee

Salem

Hair tangled
with the wind
moon dust
on my face
lover of the forest
the sea—
dark
fierce
feral things
I am an ancient soul
tempest
scarlet letter
Salem witch.

Scarlet Flowers

I want to stand in a field
of scarlet flowers
and watch you fall for me.
Undress my soul
and feel me bleed.

Falling in love
is a beautiful affliction.
It is poetry tingling
between two tongues.

Ethereal, magic, angelic.
Savage, dangerous, volcanic.

Melody Lee

Cravings

If you desire the warmth of fire
search just beneath my skin;
that's where life burns,
the heartbeat, the flame,
passion undulating within.

If you are searching for the sun;
its radiance, its glistening light,
run your fingers through my hair;
that's where She's entwined
in the silky threads I wear.

If you are looking for the moon
explore the depths of my eyes;
that's where you'll find Her
the shadow in the dark,
like Nyx, Greek goddess of the night.

If you are looking for love
probe my heart.
The more I give
the more my heart creates.
The more I am loved,
the more I make.

Look For Me

If you can't find me
in the dark,
you'll never see me
in the light.
Souls know each other
beyond sight.

Melody Lee

Archetype

I think one needs to be on the cusp
of insanity at least once in their life
to really feel the sizzling surge of creativity
throbbing inside them.
Normal is a word artists abhor,

> *even though, truth be told, sometimes everyone*
> *wants to be normal, occasionally even*
> *we crazy artsy types.*

Listen Up!

Aspiring artists—
writer, poets,
painters, potters—
don't allow bullies
to squash your spirit
or killjoys to throw water
on your fire.
Art is subjective,
always has been,
always will be.
Keep doing your thing.

Melody Lee

Morning Meditations
(in early July)

Sitting on my back porch
with my pal, my 14 year old Brussels Griffon, Samba,
or Sambalita, as I sometimes call her…she responds
to almost anything I say.

Enjoying fresh morning air, coffee and the scent
of jasmine thriving on a nearby trellis.
I am almost in a trance
from the serenity that only these early mornings offer.
I greedily accept these sunrise peace offerings.

Red cardinals and other birds, perhaps quails
or mourning doves, entertain me. So sweetly hypnotic they
serenade, then dart away, much like love that comes but
doesn't stay.

Beside me, my literary flavor of the week,
Mary Oliver's "Devotions,"
and my iPhone, volume muted.
The temptation to check my Twitter feed,
Instagram, Facebook, gnaws at me
I feel weak this early—
But I won't and I'm not and don't pick up my phone,
because I am determined to savor the euphoria
of this lovely rare moment.

Although this serene bliss won't last as the sun
begins dominating the sky, and heat
and humidity steal aurora's sensuality,
it is perfect here now, in the early hours of July.
Peaceful.
And I am getting lost, kind of high actually,
in the solitude, the simplicity of dawn.
Looking, listening, observing, as poets often do.

Red cardinals continue to appear,
and I wonder if my father and my brother
and all the kindred souls I have lost in my life
are making grand gestures. I've read that red cardinals
are a sign from a departed loved one. Silly? Perhaps.
Still, I imagine my beloveds are watching me,
reassuring me they are not only fine,
but together, laughing, loving,
maybe ice skating, gardening or playing the accordion,
making art and calligraphy; those activities they enjoyed,
in another dimension.

Melody Lee

Wisdom

A key ingredient
for an extraordinary life
is to realize nothing is ordinary
and most everything is breathtaking.

Lionhearted Woman

She is small in stature
but don't be fooled,
she's warrior strength.
You can't break a girl
that has walked through fire
and dances in storms.

Melody Lee

The Howl

He said no need for me to be a wolf
and I sensed his fear. My teeth are sharp,
my bite sinks deep. I don't roam
with the sheep or fly with the flock,
but when I love I am loyal almost to a fault
and will fight to the death for those
whom I love. Test me and you will see.

Soar

Love helps you soar.
It doesn't tie you down,
hold you back or clip your wings.
No, that's not love, my dear.

Melody Lee

Firefly

She spits gunpowder
and glitters like all the silver stars.

Intimacy

Yes, knowledge is power, but so are wisdom, courage, honesty, kindness, empathy, patience, imagination... and love. Far from being a weakness, there is magnanimous strength in being a kind and compassionate person. Being genuinely kind will empower you mentally, spiritually and emotionally, just as love does. Love does not hold captive; it is uncontainable, boundless, and there is nothing more liberating than that. I always find more strength in love, the giving and receiving, than the holding back. *Love is fire. Love is wild and fierce and free. Love is whatever you want it to be, as long it's felt in the heart, genuine and without chains and shackles.*

Get intimate with your inner self. Your soul is waiting patiently for that one-on-one relationship. Nurture and embrace the intimate gift of love you harbor within.

Melody's Fairytales

My fairytales aren't made
of desperate girls being rescued
by handsome spoiled princes.
My stories are made of badass women
teasing monsters and running wild with dragons.

Bedtime Stories

Bedtime stories read to children
Rocking them to sleep
Comforting them—
Goodnight Moon
Curious George
The Hungry Caterpillar
Where the Wild Things Are
Fables intended to deliver sustenance
wisdom
a moral compass
And here I am trying to catch fireflies
as they flicker truths in my words
a cool flow in the night air
lighting up like lanterns in a charcoal sky.

Each star is a glowing moonflower
and the sky is their garden.
Each moonflower is a poem
in the storybook of night.

Section II

Wildflower Moon

The Mountains

I go to the mountains to regroup,
when I am losing my balance,
losing myself.
I go to the mountains
and I am closer to the stars;
I breathe them in like they are a part of me.
I let them light up my lungs and float
under my skin.
I leave the mountains more alive,
pulse recharged, breathing better,
seeing clearer. I always find God
in the mountain ranges and I return to them
when I need to reclaim Her again.

Melody Lee

Fear of Flying

I flew to Philly to meet his parents,
to be with him, to see the city and watch him smile.
I met him in the airport wearing my new dress
and black knee high boots. It was my winter break...
and it was *seriously* winter in Philly.
Snow every day. Floridians aren't accustomed to snow,
and no Christmas tree or festive decorations
left an odd, almost hollow, chill in my bones
and an ache for home.

We ate bagels in the morning and had sex
in the afternoons, when his father was at work. Unlucky for
us, his step mom was always lurking somewhere in their two-
story house. I missed how he played guitar for me back home,
typically something by Led Zeppelin, The Beatles or Paul
Simon.

We took the subway to NYC, my first time for both.
I fell in love...with the lights, the fast pace, the energy, NYC
and Jewish delis. He showed me Vassar, where he graduated
with a degree in Philosophy.

I met his friends, got drunk, puked. We skied in the Poconos,
my first time on skis. I sucked. Ice did not agree with my feet.
My balance wasn't right, on the ice or with him. His father
was stern. He didn't like me. His step mom heard us banging
and my non-Jewish moaning didn't win her approval.

Awkward. I didn't like her, but I adored his mom. She gave me "Fear of Flying," by Erica Jong, and that has stayed with me all these many years later.

Melody Lee

Long Time

Make sure they are
the lightning to your thunder,
the flame to your fire,
the sun to your shine,
before committing forever;
that's a long time to be
with someone who doesn't
move your soul.

Soul Connection

Despite what the poets say,
we need more than merely mind connection,
we need chemistry and even physicality,
but above all, if our souls don't connect
nothing else will mesh.

You deserve the kind of love
that understands your gestures,
your eyes, your silence. Not the kind
that needs every single thing spelled out.
You deserve a love that understands
what you're not saying, and what you
are saying between the lines, the kind that knows
when to look at you and read your lips or eyes.
You need that soul connection kind of love,
and if your person doesn't know your soul by now,
you are with the wrong one.

Genuine soul connections
are the real aphrodisiacs.

Melody Lee

Conversations with the Moon

I like conversing with the moon
during the magical parts of midnight,
and I often wonder if She held all
of the world's intimate thoughts, secrets, fears,
and everything else we share with Her
between midnight and 4 a.m., if She'd
collapse to the ground with the weight of it all.

> *My soul and the moon*
> *are nighttime lovers.*

Fragmented Star

I didn't look for you, didn't search.
You were the furthest from my mind
and the last thing my heart expected.
Blame it on the Universe; Her conspiracy.
She brought our souls together
and would not cease until our hearts touched.
Perhaps we are of the same fragmented star
and the Cosmos wanted to attach us back together.

Melody Lee

Bohemia

Oh, those dreamy
eclectic
spontaneous
adventurous
sun-kissed
messy hair
artsy
bookish
bohemian types!

Edelweiss

Lavender clouds float like waves
in the 5pm sky
as we pull his Harley to the side
of this sleepy mountain road to stretch our legs.
We pick edelweiss, ironically the mountain flower
symbolizing deep love and devotion,
and spot a family of deer.
He is not a hunter, would never kill for sport.
He reiterates this fact to me, saying he
doesn't understand the pleasure in killing.
I am so connected to this gentle brute of a man.
I am in awe of his raw, tender masculinity.
We make dandelion wishes, capturing the moment
in our smartphone cameras,
stealing soft kisses between shoots.
I'm in love with his mouth, his laughter,
his incredibly calming voice.
I am in love with the open road
and the scent of him.
I don't ever want to lose this moment
where summertime plays and beauty breathes.
So I make my wish and hope it comes true.

Melody Lee

August Lightning

Raindrops splatter
like miniscule missiles
on my bedroom window
jolting me from a soft slumber.
I love the soothing sound of rain
in the morning,
and thunder is my companion.
A harvest of summertime warmth
fills the room.
My sleepy eyes gradually open.
Arms, legs, back…I stretch like a cat.
Morning smells...coffee, rain
and his body curled next to mine,
the scent of his skin
my favorite aphrodisiac.
I watch him sleep and reminisce
of our playful time last night,
how his greedy mouth, tongue,
teeth consumed all of me.
My body became some alien creature.
Unrecognizable animal noises erupted
from the bottom of my throat
my larynx
legs, neck, arms, stomach
contorted and twisted.
I am unknown even to me,
but he knows me well.

He brings out the beast and the best
in me. I am his lightning.
We are electricity.
August has arrived with a storm;
walls shaking,
bodies quivering,
bed sheets wet with morning dew.
The air surrounding us
electric, yet soothing,
Our heat brewing existence back
into our lifeless bones,
two lovers in full bloom, heartbeats,
and the perpetual contradiction of life itself.

Melody Lee

Love and Madness

Some relationships are clean cut and bone dry—
A plan for everything. Tidy. Perfect.
Crimp free, lacking sparks and spontaneity.
A gilded cage built on safety and monotony.
Some relationships are extravagant
and wonderfully freeing—
adventurous, late night walks under the moon,
conversations lasting for hours, unplanned trips
to anywhere. Wild. Flames. Fire.
Choose wisely. Some hearts are not meant
for this kind of exquisite madness.
Other hearts can't live without it.

Love Part II

Love can be complicated,
full of ups and downs,
twists, slips, wrong turns,
pain, growth;
it's a glorious affliction,
chaotic bliss.
Love is different things
for different people,
and yet it's the same,
because love is universal
and by design is unlimited.
But one thing love should
never be is half-ass.
You're either in it
all the way or you're not.

Melody Lee

People Skills

I like learning about people, the psyche.
Sometimes, I will look at them when they are unaware.
I'll observe and stare and see things they
don't necessarily want you, me or anyone to see.
I've been enthralled ever since, Mrs. Whidby,
my high school dance teacher gave the class
an assignment to go to the mall, find a place to sit,
and simply…people watch. I am not stalking.
Or am I? I am wicked like that. People spying is bloody cool
insight into the human soul, and I'm intrigued by human
psychology—what arouses
and inspires them, their dark and their light,
behind the veils, their naked truths exposed.
Learning about people teaches me more about me.

Translucent

Your eyes became remarkably
colorful when we talked that day
after our hike through the Sedona Red Rocks...
animated, a rainbow emerging from a dark ocean
of grief. There was an energy surrounding you,
unlike any before. And I envisioned you
with translucent wings,
graceful,
powerful,
astral,
gliding above the clouds.
Finally happy. Forever free.

Melody Lee

Abrupt Mortality

Your death—
sudden
abrupt
stole you from this life
no chance for goodbyes.

I miss the blue poppies in your eyes,
those little hidden smiles,
how they comforted me.
The solace that you were.
The joy of loving you as daughters do, robbed.
Where is the finality in this unexpected darkness?

I am not prepared for the grief,
this abyss consuming my days.

Daddy, my life forever changed.
Death has choked out your beautiful light.
I stagger in confusion. What do I do without you?

My life must go on, of course, but now
there is a large black hole. A missing part,
emptiness, vacancy.

I have lost the only person who has always,
no matter what, loved me unconditionally,
who has loved me more than anyone else ever has,

who has seen all my ugliness and only ever saw it
as beauty, who has seen my flaws only as perfections.
A piece of my soul is forever gone.

And the days are murky without your presence.
Oh death, I have felt your sharp claws
And though I know it must be
I am not a fan of abrupt mortality.

Melody Lee

Heavy

I was exhausted.
This hellish earth
weighed me down.
The cruel heaviness
of lost love,
missed chances,
goodbyes never said,
(*Daddy, I didn't know you were dying.*
How could I have when you and mom and Ken
were in denial of your illness's reality?
I was in South Florida, during Hurricane Ivan,
separated by many miles.
I knew not a thing, until it was too late.)
evaporated ashes turned dust.

My soul is a sponge
soaking up visceral emotions.
I feel everything in the marrow
of my bruised bones.
I am certain the sun will rise again,
but for now, I must weep
in my pillow
until my eyes shut tight,
until I feel the warmth
of sweet sunlight again.
The empath must rest, renew,
and rise again. This will be

my final resurrection.

Don't judge me for the way I feel things…
I never claimed to be a simple girl.

Melody Lee

Forgiveness

Forgive yourself for past blunders.
Make peace with yourself, your perfect imperfections
and all of you. Love yourself. You are in a state
of perpetual growth, evolving, blooming.

And in the letting go I found freedom.

Magic

You may store it somewhere
for a while, tuck it away,
hide it like a secret,
forget about it…
until it's needed again,
maybe unaware you are capable
of being magic and doing the miraculous,
but you *are* magic; it is yours forever.
Nobody can take that from you. Ever.
Your effervescent sparkle will materialize
at just the right time, when you need it most.
Allow magic to swim in your veins
like sea glitter.
No one can steal your shine from you.
No one.

Melody Lee

Fear

Fear will steal your power, if you let it.
Fear will eat you alive; it will choke the life
out of you, squeeze your guts, give you headaches
and heartburn, then spit you out.
You might as well be empowered, take the plunge
and do those things that scare you most,
because you are going to die anyway.
Don't make fear your slow
aching
torturous
death.
Die of liberation, not cowardice.

I moved away to a city far
from my hometown, fresh out of college.
I knew no one. This was the most
empowering thing I did for myself at age 21.
I grew the most and became the woman
I was destined to be.

I went skydiving many years later.
Jumping tandem from an airplane
is not something for everyone,
but for me it was another moment
of liberation. I was scared shitless,
but I had to do it and jumping
from that plane set me free!

Find your thing, whatever it is,
face your fear and fucking conquer it.

Are You Truly Living?

You can't pursue your life path relying on guarantees. If your heart is humming a tune that no one else hears and you feel an unstoppable force, a movement growing like sea flowers in your bloodstream, then go, be vulnerable. Sizzle! Passion means you are alive! This is your lifeline. Open your mind to magic and love. Anything is possible, nothing is guaranteed. So what! You must live this short life you are given. You must feel heat surging in your soul, a phoenix rising. Embrace your inner eagle wings, regardless of any guarantees. Otherwise, are you truly living?

Pineal Gland

The sound of my children's laughter
Their smiles. Looking into their eyes
Running my hands through their hair
Everything that makes them genuinely happy

Fresh air
The mountains
Sedona
Santa Fe
NYC
Night sky
Autumn Leaves
Rain – Clouds - Thunderstorms
Grass between my toes
Hugging trees
Hiking Trails
Outdoor sounds
Saltwater and the Ocean
The moon, in all its glorious phases
The Big Dipper
Constellations

Good music
Poetry without clichés
Discovering new poets
Writing
Yoga

Melody Lee

Orgasms that make my toes curl
and stars fall from the ceiling

When asked what nourishes
and opens my pineal gland or third eye.

Blue

I'm tired of the sky
between us. I want
to bring you coffee
in the morning
and butter your toast
with my love.
I'm tired of reaching
for the stars every night
only to reach in the dark,
alone, without you.
I'm tired of talking to the moon
instead of you. I want to put
my hand on your heart
and feel it beat for me.
I want to see and feel every color
of you, instead of all this blue
from missing you.

Melody Lee

You

Because I know you exist,
no other man will do.
The heart wants what it wants,
and mine wants you.

Nighttime Euphoria

I'm the type of girl who opens windows
on cool starry nights. Fresh air, the stars,
the moon; my night time euphoria, my tranquility.
They simultaneously invigorate and calm my soul.
This desire to feel the sky on my skin
and breathe it in while I sleep can't be controlled,
and why would I want to when I am at one
with Gaia, Mother Earth?

Melody Lee

Gaia

I run to Mother Earth
arms wide open,
and there is calm,
my comfort,
my serenity.
She never fails me,
never judges,
never rejects.
Gaia embraces all of me,
and I vow to honor all of her,
always.

Survival

Try not to be dismayed if you find her
dancing under a blazing afternoon sun.
She cares not who sees her or what they think,
she is preoccupied with feeling the wind
twisting in her rebel-red hair
and embracing the earth beneath bare feet.
You see, she carries the weight of the world
on her back. To lose herself in an infinite sky
for a time is how this free-spirited girl survives.

Moon Gypsy

Melody Lee

Soul Kiss

When you kiss my lips
do you taste my soul
or do you taste the salt
of my flesh?

Her Essence

Stop using your hands so much with her
and start using your mind, genuine words,
caring gestures…actions without conditions.
Connect with her mentally, spiritually:
seduce her soul first and foremost. Hands alone
will never reach her on a deeper level.
Unless you touch her in places your body cannot,
you are only setting yourself up
for disappointment. Once she feels that stronger,
safer connection, she will crave every part of you: mind,
body, and soul, and she will never
get enough of your physical touch.

He knew her skin by heart, so why
is it he could never reach her soul?

Melody Lee

Cereal

That time I woke at 2:30 a.m. and ate cereal
in our bed. That time you told me to turn
off the light and go back to sleep.
These were my thoughts at that moment...

Cereal or ice cream
or affection, sometimes I want all three,
when I wake up hungry, unable to fall
back to sleep. Don't tell me
not to eat in bed. Don't tell me
not to subdue pangs of hunger
in my stomach...or in my head.
I sometimes suffer with insomnia.
I toss and turn. I need to read.
I need to write. I need to walk
to the window and stare
at my cosmic lover, the moon
and count the glowing stars.
A crazy ride in the middle
of the night.

Grab a bowl, a spoon, and join me
for cereal at 2:30 a.m.

Nocturnal Clouds

You'll always be my lovely dark forest,
my favorite winter,
my melancholy moon.
I'll always tuck you tenderly
in the crevices of my heart.

> *Poets are otherworldly;*
> *they live in their heads*
> *and stagger in their towering dreams.*

Girls Are Not Machines

The best way to warm a woman, to draw her into you, is to connect with her. Talk with her and really listen when she speaks. Look her in the eyes, be attentive. Be interested. Be sincere. The best way to lose a woman is to only need her when you lust for her. Acting childish, like a pouting boy, puts a barricade up so large you will need to work extra hard to get her into your bed, if that is the goal. The appeal is in your masculinity, your ability to be strong when you feel like being weak. Your pheromones should ooze respect, trust, chivalry, manliness. This is the allure, the scent of aphrodisiac. Most women don't want perfection, flaws add character and charm; they make you human. Own your imperfections. You are interesting for having them. But no woman wants to have sex with a child, think about that before you act like a spoiled little boy who didn't get his way. It will be difficult sweeping her into your arms with an attitude like that. She feels your energy, believe me, a woman knows when you are being passive aggressive. When you do not talk with her for hours on end, slam doors, and exhibit other facetious behavior, then expect her to warm like melted butter when you touch her body, her breasts; how ludicrous a thought. Some men can be so clueless, they seem to think snapping their fingers will make her wet. Dear Sylvia, you were spot on.

Never Too Late

You settled for too long,
but it's never too late
to realize your worth
and you deserve
more…than just settling.

Melody Lee

Eye Roll

I am chaotic,
but I am settled in my ways.
Don't roll your eyes,
that is my job.

Born

I was born to chase peace
and love wild things.
I was born a beautiful
bohemian paradox.

My blood type is wild. I can't be tamed.

Section III

Black Widow

Red Lipstick, Black Stilettos

I love red
as in wine,
tulips, poppies,
and summer sunsets.

I love black
as in coffee, cats,
lingerie,
and the night.

Melody Lee

Fairytales and Swords

Once upon a time
a menacing vulture
disguised as Eros
stumbled upon a heart
so soft, bare, vulnerable
and cursed it to fall
helplessly in love.
However, the unadulterated love
in her heart
protected her from evil
casting upon her powers to ward off
demons and devils and sinister things.
Her heart, swindled by deception,
became beautifully vibrant
and strong.
Her fingertips became serpents,
her tongue a poisonous blade.
She turned her anguish into swords and steel
and spit the hideous vulture back into oblivion
where he belonged.

> *Love in your heart overpowers evil.*
> *Love conquers all.*
> *Love always wins.*

Rabbit Trap

He said he'd be my Mad Hatter
if I'd be his Wonderland.
How does a lover of tea parties,
rabbit holes and fairytales,
with a soft spot
for lunacy
refuse that?

Melody Lee

Between the Lines

She hides insanity so eloquently
between stanzas. Only a madman
could read between the lines
and understand her mind's dark abyss.

Regrets

The second worst thing I ever did
was invite a coward into my heart
and let him get comfortable there.
The worst thing I ever did
was let him stay there too long.
People say don't have regrets.
I am clinging to mine…they are
reminders of what tried to kill me.
They are my protection now.

Melody Lee

Garden

Love is a sumptuous garden
with velvet thorns and blooming vines,
honeydew and decadence.
Love is vulnerable and powerful;
it hurts and heals,
it clings and claws,
it bites and burns,
it perfects and grows wings.
Love is freeing, majestic,
spiritual, eternal.

Beast

There is a beast in all
of us that wants to be loved.

Melody Lee

Cake

He wanted me
and the cake, too.
I let him have the cake
as I crushed his overweight ego
into the marble floor
sauntering toward the window
like Rapunzel
letting down her hair to escape
the tower and never return.

Blindfold

Ashamedly, he had a way of beguiling me,
of making me believe his villainous fabrications.
I thought I was attuned to bad energy,
those unscrupulous vibes. Adorned with charm,
pathological liar. Slick I suppose…his words
felt good. I wanted to believe. I needed to. I was
in love with him. I take responsibility
for the elegant fitted blindfold I willingly wore.
Surely there were some truths in what I was fed,
or am I just being hopeful that every word
uttered from his forked tongue was not derived
from mud? My intuitive skills disappeared,
abracadabra, just like that.

Melody Lee

Liar

When he committed to love her,
cherish her, promise to be with her always...
protect her heart for God's sake,
she took all that literally. Silly woman.

Lasso

You lassoed her in with all the right words,
but your fears kept you apart. How long do you
expect a woman to wait? Life moves on
and eventually she did, too.

> *Behavior is communication*
> *and she read you loud and clear.*

Melody Lee

Sham

She fell head over heels in love
with a dream, an illusion,
what he manipulated her to believe.
He was exciting, his deception sweeter
than decadent chocolate and Dom Perignon.
It all felt so good, so comfortable, real.
He had a way with words like no other,
squeezing, pulling, twisting her heart.
It took years for her to wake
from the dream and break free from the sham.
And that's okay, it's never too late to see the fool
for what he is and the facade for what it was.
It's never too late to realize your worth.
You deserve so much better.
Walk away. It will hurt like hell
because your love was genuine.
You poured your heart into a lie,
but you will be fine, you will recover,
you will heal.

You will find out how much stronger you are,
than he ever was or ever will be.

Actor

Your theatrical words no longer
affect me because I love myself
more than your grandiose lies,
your delusions, your misguided soul.

> *You were unmistakably the most*
> *brilliant actor I've known.*

Melody Lee

Rotten Apple

You abused her heart
for too long,
tossed it around
with habitual lies, filthy deceit
as if it was a play thing, a toy.

But she thanks you, dear,
for the hypocrisy,
the manipulation.
She grew from the slime
you nourished her with.
Rose and bloomed,
a dragon flower
with coral claws.

She leaned on herself,
found the strength
to bury your name
where it belongs
deep down in the grave.

You are desperate, weak.
You no longer fool her.
You no longer have any power
over her.

Now, I want you to pray

real hard, because when the mask
peels away and the black fly
behind your cataract eye is revealed,
you are going straight down
where you are better suited,
dining on the flesh
of white maggots and worms.

> *You thought she couldn't*
> *bloom without you.*
> *She became a fucking dynasty.*

Melody Lee

Unclean

Your voice was slithery like eel skin,
but mostly reminded me of a hound dog.
Because I loved you, I told you it was smooth
and turned me on. It was never your voice
that did it for me. It was always the sweet duplicity
you made me swallow and I believed. At the time.
Now I feel dirty. Filthy. I have taken 269 showers,
at least, since the 90 days we parted, and I am still unclean.

Burn

He'll try burning you for turning him away.
But you *are* the fire that burns
and the lighthouse shimmering far and wide.
He's the moth, that darkly thing.
He can't touch your kind of flame,
he's got no power over your intoxicating magic.

> *Love is a fire,*
> *but it will not burn you,*
> *not if it's real.*

Melody Lee

Death Stalker

Mess up my sheets
not my head.
Shatter my bed
not my heart.
Lest I will have to paralyze
you when the lights go out.
Don't make me release
my venomous neurotoxin.

Spider Web

I collect deceptive men and hold them hostage
in my silk garden of sable roses and dead lilies,
I make them attend formal mushroom tea parties
and teach them how to sip elegantly.
My handsome dark knight was no exception.
In fact, he was my favorite. Sumptuous and tasty,
I licked every morsel of his velutinous lies
– mmm delectable they were –
with my sticky webbed tongue.
He pleasured my soul with his deviant darkness
as I cast an eternal spell on him.
I loved him for that, the more diabolical,
the hungrier I became. He satiated my dark desire
and honed my craft. Don't fuck with me,
I am a black widow voodoo witch.

It's all fun and games until she
kisses you with Cupid's venom
and you become trapped
in her sticky lover's web.

Melody Lee

Black Widow

Madness looks riveting
on her gothic silhouette—
Her voluptuous body
and long slender legs
adorn a black pearl Victorian gown
as lustrous cascades of silver and black
weave through her diaphanous hair,
sacredness burning in her pointed nails
red voodoo spilling
from blood thirsty lips.

Caviar and Tea

She drips feverish love
drowns in cavernous seas
royalty devouring tragedy
like caviar and tea
her majesty is having
an intimate affair with insanity.

Melody Lee

Kiss

Sometimes the enemy
walks beside you
holds your hand
and kisses your pretty lips.

Eat the Lies, Close Your Eyes

It's easy to say don't let this or that happen. We say it to ourselves, our minds know, but it's crazy what we do when we are in love, what we allow and what we close our eyes to. We desperately try to make the relationship work, we want it to. We eat the lies and close our eyes to the truth.

Melody Lee

Serpent

I always thought people who
risked their lives by playing
with poisonous snakes
were beyond crazy,
until I realized I had been
feeding one my heart every day.

Hiss! Hiss!

Snakes didn't stop hissing, they just learned how to call you "babe, bro and friend" while hiding their hiss in your presence. Often times we are blinded by deception because of the love in our own hearts. This is where you call upon your intuition and open your third eye. You'll be surprised at the snakes suddenly appearing in plain sight. Also the strength you have to ward them off.

Intuition

And with some people
I see their beaming auras,
feel their healthy energy,
their authenticity,
and I want nothing more than to stay.
Other people, I see the true nature
of their hearts and have no choice
but to walk away.

A skill I've acquired
from biting a few bad apples.

Warrior

You can wish it away all you want...you can wish it never happened, you never met, you never fell, you never took that risk, you never kissed Cupid, but all the wishing in the world won't change the fact that whatever it was that hurt you happened. So the only option you have is to celebrate the lesson. Understand that there was something valuable in the experience, even if you don't yet see that; otherwise the Universe would not have brought you there. You handled it the best you could at the time, you made it out alive. You learned. You healed. You grew. You are indeed a warrior.

I stumble, therefore I learn and grow.

Karma, Baby

Karma often takes its time
arriving slowly like a long stroll
in the park. She'll mask herself
for a while and hide
until she knows the time is just right.
Sometimes she'll play in the dark
or be apparent in the light, but karma
can't possibly keep herself from happening.
Eventually all things up will fall down;
it's the law of gravity, and it's also the law of karma.

> *I am sorry your heart was split open*
> *and for all the pain you are now enduring,*
> *but manipulative lover, liar, coward,*
> *perhaps karma has made her way back to you.*

Melody Lee

Liberated

I read your words
as fresh ink
burned the pages,
scorching my eyes…
Wide
open.
I no longer see a fragile girl
tattooed in soft skin.
I see a wounded young woman
tainted by deception,
bruises staining her heart,
flames on her fingertips,
disguised behind a veil
of black mascara and collagen lips.
You picked up a pen, dear woman,
and heard a voice
guiding you; it was your own.
Bold.
Powerful.
You found your way to freedom.

Pain into Art

I knew all these emotions would transform
into something remarkable and powerful because
of all the hurt. One can't experience that much pain and not
have it become something incredibly beautiful.

I was your Melody. You were my nightmare.

Quill and Blade

Be careful how you treat a writer.
Her pen is her weapon, her writing her sword.
She won't hesitate protecting those she loves,
including herself.

Writers don't need pointed teeth to bite
and they don't need sharp claws to scratch.
They have words and those are all the blades
they need.

> *I will either kiss you or kill you*
> *in my next book of fables and fairytales.*
> *You decide your fate, as I refill my pen.*

Amputate

"Set me free," I begged the demon
disguised as a lover and a friend,
but there is no pleading with the devil,
so, I sharpened my sword
and severed the fucking chain.

C'est La Vie

And one day I just stopped writing you
into my dreams, my plans, my future.
And life went on merrily without you.
Eventually you realize what a joke it all was
and you learn to let go of the fairytale.

I am the Spider in this Story

Don't blame the spider for attacking
when the fly deserved every bit of her venom.

Section IV

Rebirth

Slave

Some days
my words are sugar;
ripe to the ear,
sweet on the tongue,
caramel apples,
cotton candy.
Some days
they are teeth;
ferocious,
hungry,
a jackal,
carnivore,
wild beast.
But I'll be damned
if all these words
haven't made a slave
of me.

Melody Lee

Naked Clothing

No mask please.
Don't pretend.
You're more beautiful
in your authentic skin.

You look most dashing
in your soul attire.

Ohm

Close your eyes
Switch off internal chatter
Open your mind
Remove inside clutter
Difficult at first
Train your mind
Practice
Solitude
Peaceful
Soul cleansing
It will happen
Sit still
Listen
Take time to hear the earth sing
the soul's divine laughter.

Melody Lee

Enigma

Quiet soul
serene like soft rain
screaming mind
frenzied hurricane
eyes
nocturnal, dark
shape of the moon
a glowing veil
hiding
ever present
a smile like tropical sunshine
lighting paths
melting hearts
an intricate mosaic of art
nightingale
dove
sliver of paradise
enigmatic love
poetic paradox.

Candle

It can be a brutal, often dark,
sometimes tragic, lonely world,
the realm in which we humans reside,
but I am determined to be a candle
delivering hope to the hopeless,
even if only in glimmers,
even if only through poetry and prose
sent as messengers.
Love, compassion, empathy,
these emotional energy fields
are doorways of the soul
releasing our truths,
our own empowering and miraculous light.
We can never be alone as long as we
know and hold to this inner wisdom.

*We are never alone when we
carry love in our hearts.*

Melody Lee

Globe

You have the world map
traced in the palm of your hands
and the Universe swirling everywhere
inside the nucleus of you,
electrifying your essence.
You are your own archeological expedition.

Searching elsewhere, however, is not a waste
because your journey is part of the process,
the growth and what ultimately will bring you
back to your authentic self.
The questions you are desperately seeking,
the riches you are looking for,
the knowledge you are acquiring,
the continual quest…
All these mysteries reside in you.

Take a breath or two or three.
Look to yourself. The answers are there.
The treasures are there. Your castle is there.
Everything is there,
shuddering inside of you. Magic.

Had you not wandered in the dark, fallen down
gotten lost, you would not have discovered
this powerful truth.

Human

I see you, the girl holding grudges,
malevolence sticking to your skin like tree sap.
What happened to your warrior soul, your empress spirit?
That's not the way of enlightenment.
Goddesses don't store bitterness in their bones.
Snap out of it and put your glorious badass coat
back on.

> *You will make mistakes in your beautiful life;*
> *it means you are alive. Don't let your mistakes*
> *define you, don't let them bring you down.*
> *We fall, we get back up, we rise, we learn*
> *and grow. It's called being human.*

Melody Lee

Breaking

Beautiful, naked, bare hearts
trust easily
fall fast
crash hard

suffer the most
because they are willing to tear
rip
shatter
crush
break
repeatedly
for those whom they love

and like a depleted muscle
those same hearts heal
thicker
tougher
stronger

becoming more durable
pliable
open
vulnerably alive
courageous
receptive to love
…receiving and giving.

Be gentle with yourself while healing,
and be prepared for the discovery
of tremendous strength.

Unkindred

Some people are stone cold
even your fire won't warm them.
Icy temperatures, frigid hearts,
bitter language, fake smiles. . .
These disunited souls don't mesh
with free spirits. Send them love,
say a prayer, wish them well
and stroll along.

At Peace

There was a time
I clutched darkness
and devoured empty kisses.
These days, I inhale dawn's light,
while enchanting morning sounds
serenade me.
I am perfectly peaceful,
kissed by nature's music,
bluebirds, daffodils
and the golden rays of a smiling sun.

Melody Lee

Kindness

They think you are fragile
because you are kind, as if kindness
is a deficiency causing one to be frail
and flawed. They haven't felt the flame
beneath your skin, surely they would
flee if they did. They haven't
seen the beast behind the warmth
of your eyes, they would freeze if they did.
And they haven't visited the sharp edges
of your mind, else they would bleed.
Kindness is a great strength; it fools people
into thinking you are weak, and is it not the fool
who holds the lesser power?

Don't mistake her gentle spirit or tender heart.
She is full of fire. She can be dainty
and still have claws. She can be sweet
and still make flames. That is her magic.

Self-talk

Sometimes your kindness and generous spirit
are unappreciated. Do not let that harden you,
do not let it make you bitter or resentful.
Your deeds do not go unnoticed. The Cosmos
is always observing, listening and bringing you
what you need, when you need. The right people
will come into your life, even if only for a short while,
the right lessons will be learned, and the timing
will be as it should.

In the growth process, there will be hurts
and betrayals; that is just part of living a full life.
Everything is in accordance with the evolution
of your soul. Learn to trust the lessons,
even when you don't understand the whys
or reasons behind them.

In time, those experiences become clearer
and you realize they were necessary
to grow as a human being. The path
is being opened allowing better things
to enter your life. *Believe.*

Melody Lee

Show Me

Show me who you are beneath the flowers
and the smiles and the masks you wear
every day. I want to nurture your dark side
and dance in fields of black orchids
with you. I want to kiss your sadness
and swallow your tears. Let me taste your sins
and carry your burdens. I will store your secrets
inside the depths of my heart,
safe, secure, where they will never part.

No More Tears

You think you'll never get over that one love, that one you cried pails of tears for—caught midstream on your front yard as your neighbors walked by. Then there is the embarrassing breakdown in the insurance office, and that time you impulsively cut all your long silky hair in your attempt to *prove* something; what I had no idea. And don't forget those many lost nights of sleep. Then…you go off to university, get involved with student life, meet someone, graduate, move away, start a career, get married, have children…and one day, years later, you stop in your tracks and realize you barely ever think of him anymore. You can't even recall the last time he popped in your mind, but when he does, it's always with a smile.

Melody Lee

Self-Love

I fell out of love with him
and he thought I fell in love
with someone else. I did.
I fell in love with me.

Picking up the Pieces

The right one will come behind you
and pick up the pieces you thought
weren't worth picking up, and love
the parts you thought weren't lovable.

Suspenders and Astronomy

He walked in the crowded room with an unlit cigarette hanging from his mouth, half tucked and unbuttoned shirt showing off his tanned, chiseled chest. He wore dark suspenders and was in desperate need of a haircut. He seemed a little off, as if he'd rather be anywhere but here, among strangers. He was rough around the edges and had calm eyes, pale blue and sharp, and he smiled the most intriguing, crooked smile.

When he looked at me, I couldn't seem to look away. And he noticed. He walked toward me, said a few words about the aura in the room, then winked, the sly kind that said this party is lame, arrogant people making shallow conversation.

We grabbed a martini, stepped outside and talked about astronomy, Charles Darwin and the decline of humanity.

He left a couple hours later without telling me his name or asking mine, but when he briefly stepped away, I picked up his phone. I think he knew. I think he expected me to look. The connection was real, seed planted, chase in motion.

I plan to surprise him with a Big Dipper text and an invite to an upcoming exhibit at the city planetarium.
He'll accept. The chase has begun.

Slipping

I knew I was falling for him
by the way my tongue tied,
words slurred,
even my eyelids blushed.

Melody Lee

Blood Dance

I craved the aching ferocity
inside his brutal poetry.
The throbbing of two souls connecting
as wet, cold blood dripped from the tips
of our pens,
pain drooling from our mouths
on parchment,
languishing in sweet liquidity.
Prose's kiss opening a dimension
inside of me,
a place I thought long gone,
as if stolen by death,
washed away after life's last
horrendous storm.
Through sheer accident, I felt life's rhythm again.
So did he.
Clouds became white pillows
and the sun began to glisten. For both of us.
Here was the miracle, the proof
of synchronicity.
We met in the darkness, the corners we chose to share,
and together we made light expand,
found hidden treasure there.

Muse

He strolled into my world
like smooth jazz in the park.
It was the end of summer
and the writer in me felt inspired
by something fresh, new.
His voice was a combination
of warm chamomile
on a snowy night and hot tamales
in the middle of July. The contradiction
had my attention, an allure irresistible
for the romantic in me. I have always loved
the deep, seductive sound of a man's voice.
His was sensual, husky, divine.
And he was just the right amount
of nerdy-intellectual for my geeky eclectic side.
Perfect for my mind's poetic cerebral hemisphere
and my thoughts were racing.
Without a second thought
I released the guard rail protecting my heart.
There's no denying he will end up
in one or two or a dozen of my short stories.
A poet needs a muse
and he may be my favorite one.

Melody Lee

Labyrinthine

Supple girl
seductive sea
half human, half ocean

Sleek siren
singing clever tales
of lost lovers and loneliness

You are the starfish swimming
in the center
of my being

The necromancer
who keeps me sane
who keeps me whole

Erotic sea witch
Sapiosexual mermaid queen.

Chocolate

I eat poetry like smooth
Godiva chocolate
savor it like fine French wine.
I need it like air.
Crave it like love.
Require it like sex.

Butterfly

In order to regain balance and appreciate the light, there will be times you must retreat to the sanctuary of your cocoon. A way to the brilliance within yourself is by searching deep internally. Indulge in the solitude and quiet of your magnificent shell. When you are ready to break out again, everything has an incandescent vibe...suddenly you burst with renewed vigor, strength that otherwise may not have been found. Don't be ashamed to withdraw back to yourself from time to time. Allow your soul to rest, and your spirit much needed growth.

You didn't know her before the butterfly days. You didn't know her as the inward, awkward, timid caterpillar. But her wild, illuminated wings were inevitable, her design and destiny. Now you know her with a gypsy heart and rebel spirit. I wonder if you'd love the dark caterpillar in her as you love the bohemian butterfly.

Voice

The weak will attempt to censor your voice. They do not want you to write your stories, sing your songs, worship differently than them, pray to gods they don't believe in—they demand you be part of the status quo. It is important for you to continue on your artistic journey, or whatever path your soul is traveling. Be steadfast—Speak your voice, follow your intuition, you have a message that needs to be heard. The strong will inspire, stand and project with you.

The fearful will try to tame you, afraid you might poison their minds and those whom they love; afraid of your wild, afraid of your strength. Like the village people who shunned the Belladonnas for what they blindly saw as witchery, because these maidens preferred the company of the forest or chose not to be married, eventually burning them for being unlike the masses. People still burn us today, but in different ways. Sadly, fear and ignorance have enslaved people.

If you have a message to convey, be it through writing, public speaking, performing, teaching, the arts, or whatever creative outlet it may be, be resolute and project your message for the edification of the world. The receptive ones will listen and walk with you. The intrepid will encourage. The evolved will comprehend your creativity, applauding your imagination. You will learn and grow together on perhaps a shared journey, enriching your lives and others.

Melody Lee

When you are being true to yourself you are winning, conquering internal inhibitions and fears. Whether or not the words you write are fiction or real, those thoughts, those feelings and emotions being expressed are coming from some place inside the recesses of your mind, heart and soul. You are an artist, a creator, a writer, a poet. And that is stripped naked soul baring authenticity in its purest form. That is your truest voice.

If you can't be true to yourself,
how do you expect
to be true to anyone else?

Happy Hour

Writing is a cocktail
of insanity and serenity.
There is always a little madness
mixed in the sweet placidity.

Melody Lee

Rebirth

A new year, a fresh start,
we hear it every year.
Same song. Same story.
The truth is, every morning
is an opportunity to begin anew.
Each day could be your first day of January,
by changing your mindset.
Why wait until the "New Year"
to chase your dreams,
to be a better person,
to be happier,
to lose weight,
stop an addiction,
or make your life better
in the way only you can...
Why wait when every day is your chance
to break bad habits and work toward your goals,
until you achieve your ultimate personal greatness.

Bravery

For those who think feeling deeply
makes one impotent, weak...wrong.
It takes courage to really open,
and feel to the core
of all your active chromosomes.
To risk excruciating heartache and pain,
again. To risk condemnation and criticism.
This kind of vulnerability is strength.
It is brave. Never let any tell you otherwise.

Melody Lee

Pieces of Me

I have a gothic soul.
I love Scottish castles,
owls, ravens and 'The Cure.'
I get melancholy, tend to be an insomniac,
have a fetish for vampires and macabre things.
I stay up late reading.
I really do like spiders, even tarantulas.
I won't kill them—
spider language intrigues me.
I prefer long walks at night
spending time with my friend, Luna,
and my favorite seasons are fall and winter.
That doesn't mean I don't love
God, Spirituality,
springtime, rainbows,
and things emphasizing the light.

Cosmic Queen

Aligned with the sun
galactic stars
and The Milky Way
free thinker
rebel and restless by nature
like all beautifully primal things
she's got the mind of an old soul poet
and the wandering spirit
of a cosmic gypsy queen.

Melody Lee

The Choice

Acknowledge shortcomings, we are human after all and not without faults, which make us intricately, stunningly complex. Refuse to dwell on the negatives; they only serve to exacerbate a pointless situation. For me, staying in a low energy field of thought only weighs me down and is toxic for those in my space. Staying inside a negative mindset for too long is poisonous. You can be a bleak graveyard, dim and dreary, or you can be luminosity blazing through the night. You can be the dead flower in a thriving garden or you can be the miraculous weed growing triumphantly in a field of dirt or through concrete. Where I focus my thought energy is where I reside mentally, so even though we need to retreat to the "forest" periodically, make a conscious effort to rise above dark gravity that seeks to pull you down.

Never let life's little mishaps
quench your fire.
Choose to be a radiant beam
of magical moonlight.

Melody

Listen for the chiming
of your heartbeat
follow its voice
unravel its tune
enigma between breaths
stillness
silence
where life and death
collide
and shadows hide
feel the currents
cadences
pulses
rhythms

The melodies of your sacred soul
hold secrets, stories
Gaia breathing in you.

Melody Lee

Dizzy

The feeling of being both trapped and free
is the most mind twisting feeling of all.

Evanesce

Don't mind me, I am a creature of habit,
and like all solitary celestial birds,
I must regain my ethereal wings and fly away.

.

Melody Lee

I Hope

I hope when you think of New Mexico
and Arizona, you feel my wild heart,
remembering the time we traveled there,
exploring ghost towns, climbing the red rock,
happy and in love
with the western part of the United States
and each other.
I hope when you look at the moon,
you remember how we would take late night walks
so that I could be closer to Her
and you.
I hope when you touch tulips and lilies,
you feel how I bloomed for you.
I hope when you read poetry you think of me.
I hope you know this poem is for you.

Breadcrumbs

Breadcrumbs of wisdom,
more valuable
than nuggets of gold,
for breadcrumbs
can be chewed,
swallowed,
devoured whole.
Breadcrumbs feed,
they nourish the mind
and ultimately the soul.
While gold may glitter,
sparkle and shine,
it is an expensive rock
to be adorned,
not absorbed,
Try consuming gold.
You will remain hungry,
never satiated,
with a deep need
for…more.

Melody Lee

Best Company

It is hard to beat the company
of solitude
and a fresh pot of strong coffee,
when I am alone
with my favorite books, pen, paper,
and keyboard sitting near me,
here
where I will
carve out the next chapter in my book
of candid short stories
and elaborate lucid poetry.

Writing Day

When you ask me what I am wearing today,
knowing it's a writing day,
I have to wonder where you think I am going.
I am a poet, it's not a glamorous profession.
Most likely I've thrown on a pair of shorts
(or jeans depending on weather) and a t-shirt,
have my hair in a ponytail and am drinking cold coffee.
I'm not dolling up for the keyboard
and I wish the coffee would stay hot.

Melody Lee

Road Trip

I'd love to take a road trip
inside the mesmeric maze
of your maniacal mind,
pack my bags and wind
around your cerebral cortex,
into the hypothalamus, all four lobes
and the hemispheres in between.
You may find me staggering
in the ventricles
of wandering, ancient cities
found deep inside the recesses
of your brainstem,
or stuck in the small pocket
of the pituitary gland.
You may even find me
surfing on ganglia practicing my fine motor skills
or making magnanimous brainwaves
crash landing on your cerebellum.
This could be dangerous,
mind shattering;
it could be mystical and spiritual enlightenment.
This could be a symptom of drowning,
being swallowed in rivers of delectable mindgasms.

Growing Pains

Be receptive to what life is teaching at any particular moment, even amidst pain and sadness. The sages know suffering ultimately gifts us with blessings, and tragedies develop us into empathetic, intuitive human beings, preparing us to do great things with our gifts. Don't be afraid of your struggles, don't fight them like I did for too long. They serve as your teachers, making you dangerously wise and wonderfully compassionate. Your battles and challenges are preparing you for magnificent strength. Allow the uncomfortable to happen, knowing that there is an abundance of power within you, waiting for you to tap into it and realize all that you are.

Your growing pains are you shedding weaknesses,
old selves, past perceptions; they are transforming you into
the enlightened woman or man you are destined
to be.

At the bottom of confusion there is clarity.
Hold to that important truth. Grasp it.
Cling to it.

Melody Lee

The Grand Adventure of Life

If I didn't have scratch marks
on my tongue or thistles
in my side, I'd be perfectly boring
and un-intriguing.
My flesh is not a perfect painting,
but it is a perfect masterpiece
created by combustions and collisions
on my life's journey.
The fact that I am now comfortable
with these jagged edges
gives me an advantage, a self-confidence
I once lacked, but my comfort
did not come without pain,
sadness, losses, trials,
and it didn't arrive overnight.
It took years to become at peace
with my mind and my body,
to know who I am inside and out.
I continue to bump into walls,
fall into rivers and crash into life,
but I understand now more than ever
that this is part of the grand adventure
in my allotted time on earth.

Castle

You kissed my soul
with magic and madness
wolf on your breath
touching me everywhere
sweet and wild.

Your heart was my castle.

Melody Lee

Happily Ever After

She is the fairytale you
write about in your story
and dream about in real life.
The one who loses her way
but finds her dashing wolf.
The one who falls madly in love
with an enchanting beast.
The one with the hopeful eyes
and happy ending.

Acknowledgements

Thank you to my husband, who cheers me on behind the scenes. Thank you for keeping things together while I write. I love you, darling. You are my rock.

My two sons, thank you for being amazing human beings and making sure I smile every single day. You both have made me a better human being. I love you more than poetic words could ever express. You are my heart, my light, and the best part of my life. Both of you.

To my mom. Thank you for giving me a loving and happy home when I was a child, for your soft and nurturing side, also for your orderly side that taught me the importance of tenacity and hard work. Thank you for loving me, even during my wild teenage years. My rebellion was not always pretty, but you were always there when I needed you. You still are. Because of you, I have beautiful stories. I love you so much.

Thank you to my dad who filled our home with books and art and music, who turned our yard into a bohemian paradise. Artistic proclivities flow in my veins, because of you. Thank you for encouraging me to follow my heart, to romance it with literature, poetry, ballet. I love you and I miss you every single day of my life.

Thank you to my brother, who is also no longer here. Your curious eyes gave me a different view of the world. Your adventurous spirit still touches me and always will. I miss you. I love you.

To Alfa Holden. Oh, Alfa, where do I begin? You have been divinely put on my path by a higher power. Of this I am sure. I don't know how I was so lucky, so blessed to meet you, but believe me when I tell you, I am a better person for knowing you. You are a treasure, and I am humbled and honored with your friendship. Thank you for reading, reviewing and writing the forward to *Season of the Sorceress*. I love you.

To Rachel Finch. Thank you for being a beautiful angel in my life. Your friendship and support of my poetry through the years means the world to me. It is an honor to call you friend and have you read and review *Season of the Sorceress*. Love you.

To Monika Carless. Thank you for your gift of storytelling and for sharing it with the world. I cannot begin to tell you how overjoyed and honored I am to have you read and review *Season of the Sorceress*. I am blessed for knowing you. Love you.

To Christine Ray. What a joy it has been getting to know you and have you as editor as I put my poetry, prose, quotes and stories into a book. Thank you for editing *Season of the Sorceress*. For your expertise. For your creative suggestions.

For your meticulous eye. And, of course, for your patience. You've been an incredible guide these past few months. I am honored to call you friend.

To Kindra Austin and Candice Louisa Daquin. Thank you both for proofreading my manuscript, for your helpful suggestions, for believing in me as an artist and a writer with a voice. Your support and encouragement mean so much to me. Thank you from the bottom of my heart.

To Nicole Lyons. Thank you for reading my first draft and for your friendship the past few years. Your support has always been held in high regard. I am grateful for you.

To Mitch Green. Thank you for taking my ideas and creating an exquisite masterpiece of a cover. Thank you for working with me until I was completely satisfied and for your upbeat vibes while I asked for another tweak here and another tweak there. I'm sure sometimes you wanted to knock me over my OCD head. Thank you for your sublime talent that brought my book together!

Thank you to my writing tribe and soul warriors who inspire me in countless ways. If I could hug each of you every day, I would.

Thank you to my readers, both online and off, who cheer me on and support me in ways you aren't even aware. I love you all.

Thank you to the independent bookstores that house my books, and a big thank you to Midtown Reader for stocking and selling my books for the past two years.

If you bought this poetry book, or any of my books, thank you so very much. I hope you enjoy my journey.

About the Author

Melody Lee is a word artist who weaves thoughts, fantasies and realities into a myriad of themes, from inspirational writing to darker poems. Her poetry ranges from love and loss, to life, growth and empowerment, written with a witchy, bohemian flair, inspired by nature, freedom and relationships. Melody is the author of two collections of poetry and prose: *Moon Gypsy* and *Vine: Book of Poetry*. She lives in Florida with her husband and two children.

Email: coda.melody@yahoo.com
Instagram: @melodyleepoetry
Twitter: @melodyleepoetry
Facebook: www.facebook.com/melodyleepoetry

Made in the USA
Middletown, DE
09 March 2019